Quotable Quotes Excellence

Vol. 3 of 20

Hope

CHARLES MWEWA

Published by:

ACP

Ottawa, Ontario

Canada

www.acpress.ca

Copyright © 2024 Charles Mwewa

www.charlesmwewa.com

ISBN: 978-1-988251-95-0

DEDICATION

For

Claudine T.

CONTENTS

AUTHOR'S WORD

Wisdom is supreme. Wisdom is grand. Wisdom is the ultimate excellence. If you want to get anything, get wisdom. The best way to be wise and to gain wisdom is to observe, and a lot of it.

Life has a pattern; words have the power to change anything. But only words which alliterate sound and meaning, and natural reality have that power – the power to see clearly, to understand complex ideas and to apply them to real life situations and be better.

The nuggets provided in this book of *Quotable Quotes Excellence, Vol. 3 of 20: Hope* (in a series of 20), are prepared for you – if you love wisdom and thinking.

cm.

HOPE, CONFIDENCE & EXPECTATION

MOSTLY HOPE

1. "Hope is the only weapon that defeats death."

2. "If hope comes between you and death, death will flee."

3. "Hope is always available in the world; your job is to find it."

Quotable Action

◀ What I learned from the quotes:

▼ What I will do with what I learned:

4. "Hope never loses you, you
   are the one who loses hope,
   instead."

5. "Where there is hope, there is
   life."

6. "Hope makes abstract
   concepts become things."

Quotable Action

◀ What I learned from the quotes:

▼ What I will do with what I learned:

7. "There is nothing that hope has failed to create."

8. "The voice of hope searches the past, saves the present, and sustains the future."

9. "First hope, then faith."

Quotable Action

◀ What I learned from the quotes:

▼ What I will do with what I learned:

10.   "Never leave hope, even if you are drowning ."

11.   "You can always find hope if you take time to look ."

12.   "You can always find hope if you are not discouraged by negative circumstances and experiences."

Quotable Action

◀ What I learned from the quotes:

▼ What I will do with what I learned:

13.　　"Hope will search heaven and hell to bring you what you agreed with it to."

14.　　"Even the strongest medicine will fail without hope."

15.　　"With hope, the future is as clear and certain as the past."

Quotable Action

◀ What I learned from the quotes:

▼ What I will do with what I learned:

16.   "Circumstances will make your life harder; hope will make it easier."

17.   "Hope will extend your years and postpone death."

18.   "Hope is neutral – it makes both bad and good come true."

Quotable Action

◄ What I learned from the quotes:

▼ What I will do with what I learned:

19.　"Where there is hope, strategies and tactics become alive."

20.　"With hope, you may lose a battle but win the war."

21.　"Kingdoms are held together by hope and destroyed by doubt."

Quotable Action

◀ What I learned from the quotes:

▼ What I will do with what I learned:

22.   "Don't give someone money before you give them hope, it'll be squandered ."

23.   "The easiest way to kill anything, is to first separate it from hope."

24.   "Hope is the last thing you must hold on to, even if all foundations are falling apart."

Quotable Action

◀ What I learned from the quotes:

▼ What I will do with what I learned:

25. "When you lose hope,
     you lose the battle."

26. "Life and hope are
     related, where there is one,
     even if it's just a bare breath,
     there is the other."

27. "Your hope must be
     closer and visible as your
     shadow, even in sunlight."

Quotable Action

◀ What I learned from the quotes:

▼ What I will do with what I learned:

28.   "Hope in the best even if the circumstances dictate otherwise."

29.   "While faith conquers the moment, hope conquers the future."

30.   "You can't see the future only if you don't have hope."

Quotable Action

◀ What I learned from the quotes:

▼ What I will do with what I learned:

31. "Hope is to a man with sight as the walking stick is to the blindman."

32. "A sailor can lose a campus but still reach her destination with hope."

33. "When all that defines you is striped off you, hope will redefine you."

Quotable Action

◀ What I learned from the quotes:

▼ What I will do with what I learned:

34.　　"Even the mighty fall,
when they lose hope."

35.　　"With hope, death is not
the end, it is the beginning."

36.　　"Faith is great, hope is
greater, and love is the
greatest."

Quotable Action

◀ What I learned from the quotes:

▼ What I will do with what I learned:

37.　　"The best plans are those which give hope."

38.　　"Hope is synonymous with a future."

39.　　"Hope is blind to directions; it is your duty to set it on the right trajectory."

Quotable Action

◀ What I learned from the quotes:

▼ What I will do with what I learned:

40. "Work must be produced by faith, labor prompted by love, and endurance inspired by hope."

41. "Hope takes the shape of its master."

42. "If your hope is in God, you will reap eternal life."

Quotable Action

◀ What I learned from the quotes:

▼ What I will do with what I learned:

43.   "You can hope in anything; hope doesn't choose whom to obey."

44.   "Hope loves those who love it; and is far away from those who doubt."

45.   "Hope all the way."

Quotable Action

◀ What I learned from the quotes:

▼ What I will do with what I learned:

46.   "If you lose hope, you
    can find it again, if you don't
    quit."

47.   "The difference between
    hope and faith; hope doesn't
    need faith, but faith does need
    hope."

48.   "Hope is neither a
    believer nor a non-believer; it's
    abeliever."

Quotable Action

◀ What I learned from the quotes:

▼ What I will do with what I learned:

49.   "Christ is the hope of glory."

50.   "Education, knowledge and enlightenment bring hope."

51.   "Like money, hope is valuable, if you don't keep it with care, it vanishes."

Quotable Action

◀ What I learned from the quotes:

▼ What I will do with what I learned:

52.　　"Hope is delicate and slippery, hold on to it unswervingly."

53.　　"Hope renews one's strength in the Lord."

54.　　"The hope of the ungodly has a future, but a bad future."

Quotable Action

◀ What I learned from the quotes:

▼ What I will do with what I learned:

55.　　"The hope of the godly is unfailing love."

56.　　"Those who have hope, praise God more and more."

57.　　"Hope in God's word, makes waiting possible."

Quotable Action

◀ What I learned from the quotes:

▼ What I will do with what I learned:

58.　"One thing hope never does for its client; it never puts them to shame."

59.　"If you already have it, don't hope for it; rather, hope for what is not."

60.　"Hope is currency, the more you have, the richer you are."

Quotable Action

◄ What I learned from the quotes:

▼ What I will do with what I learned:

61.   "If your God never gives you hope, it is a dead god."

62.   "Integrity effuses hope."

63.   "Hope saves."

Quotable Action

◀ What I learned from the quotes:

▼ What I will do with what I learned:

64.　　"On the wings of hope,
you can traverse the future
and back."

65.　　"Hope ends all fears."

66.　　"Hope speaks to
impossible situations as
though they are mundane and
tamable."

Quotable Action

◀ What I learned from the quotes:

▼ What I will do with what I learned:

67.   "A good night sleep is only possible because of hope for tomorrow."

68.   "Hope ignores the past and believes in the future."

69.   "To set your mind on things above, is to have hope."

Quotable Action

◄ What I learned from the quotes:

▼ What I will do with what I learned:

70.　　"Hope makes work
　　pleasant."

71.　　"It is the glory of men to
　　hope; it is the delight of God
　　to bring the victory."

Quotable Action

◀ What I learned from the quotes:

▼ What I will do with what I learned:

72.　　"Courage and heroism dance to the tune of hope."

73.　　"Hope for big things, bigger than your strength, and hope will work double."

74.　　"Hope does not come from the mountains; it comes from within and above you."

Quotable Action

◀ What I learned from the quotes:

▼ What I will do with what I learned:

75.   "If you don't say yes to hope, hope will say no to you."

76.   "There is a dead hope and a living hope; the later leads to true riches."

77.   "Hope gives birth post-menopause."

Quotable Action

◀ What I learned from the quotes:

▼ What I will do with what I learned:

78.　"Shadows will always hope, so long as the sun remains."

79.　"The hope of smoke is fire, that of shadow is the light, and of man, is the unseen reality."

80.　"The poor's hope is a promise of tomorrow."

Quotable Action

◄ What I learned from the quotes:

▼ What I will do with what I learned:

81.   "If you can pray, God can grant you what you hope for."

82.   "Hope for something before you pray."

83.   "Where there is hope, there is security and safety."

Quotable Action

◄ What I learned from the quotes:

▼ What I will do with what I learned:

84.　　"If you put your hope in God's never-ending love, He will delight in you."

85.　　"If you postpone hope, your heart will get sick."

86.　　"Ultimately, all mankind hope for the glory of God."

Quotable Action

◄ What I learned from the quotes:

▼ What I will do with what I learned:

87.　　"Hope is like a campus; lose it and you lose direction."

88.　　"Hope makes gods and immortals equal; with it they conquer the future."

89.　　"Anything that you allow to kill your hope, loads over you."

Quotable Action

◄ What I learned from the quotes:

▼ What I will do with what I learned:

90.   "Never go to war or be
        involved in a war without
        hope alongside you."

91.   "Give hope the first
        place in your future schedule."

92.   "Look for hope,
        everywhere."

Quotable Action

◀ What I learned from the quotes:

▼ What I will do with what I learned:

93.   "Those who have hope may go down, but they always end up above."

94.   "Hope and endurance are related; they both reach the finishing line."

95.   "Hope shines brightest when it is darkest."

Quotable Action

◀ What I learned from the quotes:

▼ What I will do with what I learned:

96.   "No matter how tough
        the task is, where there is hope
        and perseverance, there is a
        solution."

97.   "Don't write anyone off
        who has hope."

98.   "Hope and positive
        expectation are two sides of
        the same coin; you can't have
        one without the other."

Quotable Action

◀ What I learned from the quotes:

▼ What I will do with what I learned:

99.   "Hope breeds confidence."

100.   "There may be many enemies in the journey of progress, but with hope, they can all be defeated."

101.   "Hope is being confident that unseen realities are, in fact, real."

102.   "Hope and confidence are two sides of the same coin."

Quotable Action

◄ What I learned from the quotes:

▼ What I will do with what I learned:

103. "Confidence is a jacket best worn from the inside out."

104. "Confidence is a full cup concept; a conviction that repels external discouraging forces."

105. "You can lose the easiest interview, fumble on a fare project and miss a critical chance, all because of lack of confidence."

Quotable Action

◀ What I learned from the quotes:

▼ What I will do with what I learned:

106.   "Confidence defines invincibility – it flies higher than the sky and stands steadier than a rock."

107.   "In religion, it is called faith; in business, confidence."

108.   "Confidence is being certain that what you desire will come to pass."

Quotable Action

◀ What I learned from the quotes:

▼ What I will do with what I learned:

109. "Confidence is feeling of
self-assurance that you have
what it takes to succeed."

110. "Confidence first
appreciates its own abilities or
qualities and then trusts that
others will do the same."

111. "Confidence is a secure
trust that you can be and do as
well as anybody in your
specific goal."

Quotable Action

◄ What I learned from the quotes:

▼ What I will do with what I learned:

112.　"Without confidence, the likelihood of losing increases exponentially."

113.　"Confidence achieves more than it loses."

114.　"Confidence is not blind, not superstitious; it's an inner knowledge that you are capable of something."

Quotable Action

◀ What I learned from the quotes:

▼ What I will do with what I learned:

115.   "If you want it so much, build confidence for it, and it will be yours."

116.   "Confidence attracts confidantes – people and resources that bring you into your future."

117.   "You have not had it because you lack or lost confidence; re-build your brand, your capture the confidence."

Quotable Action

◀ What I learned from the quotes:

▼ What I will do with what I learned:

118.   "Anybody can get very far just with a bit of confidence."

119.   "Whatever makes you confident – clothes, hairdo, shoes, make-up, credentials, faith, looks, and etc. – do it more regularly."

120.   "The most common reason why many people drink or take drugs, is because it makes them confident."

Quotable Action

◀ What I learned from the quotes:

▼ What I will do with what I learned:

121. "Confidence is the number one selling commodity on any market."

122. "If you can accept yourself within, you can cause everything and everybody without to accept you."

123. "If you love yourself with a healthy love, you are confident."

Quotable Action

◀ What I learned from the quotes:

▼ What I will do with what I learned:

124.   "The first stage to becoming free is to accept those things about you that you think make you unacceptable."

125.   "If you can love what you think other people dislike about you, you can conquer anything."

126.   "Love who you are – your height, weight, color, tribe, race, background, and etc., and your confidence will go over the roof."

Quotable Action

◀ What I learned from the quotes:

▼ What I will do with what I learned:

127.   "Accept the things that you least expect others to accept about who you are."

128.   "You may not enter the presence of God and receive your portion without confidence."

129.   "Confidence comes to those who focus more on their inner strengths than on their external frailties."

Quotable Action

◀ What I learned from the quotes:

▼ What I will do with what I learned:

130. "If you can count your blessings and name them one by one, you'll soon realize that you have more things to be confident about."

131. "Confidence is spiritual – those who have it, will soar with wings like eagles."

132. "Remember that I have commanded you to be determined and confident. Do not be afraid or discouraged, for I, the LORD your God, am with you wherever you go."[1]

---

[1] Joshua 1:9

Quotable Action

◀ What I learned from the quotes:

▼ What I will do with what I learned:

133. "But blessed is the one who trusts in the LORD, whose confidence is in him."[2]

134. "Though an army besiege me, my heart will not fear; though war break out against me, even then I will be confident."[3]

135. "Confidence is courage, resilience, a strong resolve that what God has promised will come to pass."

---

[2] Jeremiah 17:7
[3] Psalm 27:3

Quotable Action

◀ What I learned from the quotes:

▼ What I will do with what I learned:

136.   "'With him is only the
arm of flesh, but with us is the
LORD our God to help us
and to fight our battles." And
the people gained confidence
from what Hezekiah the king
of Judah said."[4]

137.   "Great confidence has
she who trusts in God than he
who trusts in men."

---

[4] 2 Chronicles 32:8

Quotable Action

◄ What I learned from the quotes:

▼ What I will do with what I learned:

138.   "Prayer breeds confidence: 'This is the confidence we have in approaching God: that if we ask anything according to his will, he hears us. And if we know that he hears us — whatever we ask — we know that we have what we asked of him."[5]

---

[5] 1 John 5:14-15

Quotable Action

◀ What I learned from the quotes:

▼ What I will do with what I learned:

139. "At the end of every confidence, is a deep reward."

140. "Confidence eraser #1: Negative words – the easiest method known to humans to kill self-confidence and esteem. Avoid negative people or to listen (you can't avoid hearing, but you can choose not to listen) to negative words against you."

141. "Confidence eraser #2: Don't keep a record of your wrongs – remember that everyone makes mistakes, errors, and does wrong."

Quotable Action

◄ What I learned from the quotes:

▼ What I will do with what I learned:

142.   "Confidence eraser #3: Don't go on documenting your faults as if you are the first one to have done wrong. Be forgiven and move on."

143.   "Confidence eraser #4: Divorce your unpleasant past from your present and future – if possible, erase it from your memory, or at least, ignore it when it constantly batters your mind."

Quotable Action

◀ What I learned from the quotes:

▼ What I will do with what I learned:

144.   "Confidence eraser #5: If you have to remember anything about yourself or somebody else, remember the best parts. Don't live in the past and neither should you count your failures, disappointments, and miseries, etc."

145.   "Confidence eraser #6: Lack of deliberate creativity – confidence is jagged up by creative thinking and inventing. Think of ways to showcase your talents, abilities, graces, gifts, or any particularities that are uniquely yours."

Quotable Action

◀ What I learned from the quotes:

▼ What I will do with what I learned:

146.   "Confidence eraser #7:
Neglect – it is the glory of
God to give you the body,
soul, and spirit; it is your duty
to enhance their value and
usefulness by continuous
improvement."

147.   "Confidence eraser #8:
Comparisons – when you are
in the habit of comparing
yourself to others, you may
limit your confidence and do
damage to your self-esteem."

Quotable Action

◀ What I learned from the quotes:

▼ What I will do with what I learned:

148.   "Confidence eraser #9: Fixation on your assumed blameful areas – even the most beautiful woman and the most handsome man has areas they wish they did not have. Fixation on small areas of imperfection can damage your overall constitution. Accept who you are and what you have and move on."

149.   "Confidence eraser #10: Lack of cultivation – literally and figuratively, can damage your self-esteem in the long run. Weed yourself out and prune yourself often."

Quotable Action

◀ What I learned from the quotes:

▼ What I will do with what I learned:

150.   "God told Joshua to have two qualities if he was to conquer Jericho: Ambition (determination) and confidence, thus, 'Remember that I have commanded you to be determined [ambitious] and confident.' And then God defined ambition (determination) and confidence, 'Do not be afraid or discouraged, for I, the LORD your God, am with you wherever you go.'"[6]

---

[6] Joshua 1:9

Quotable Action

◀ What I learned from the quotes:

▼ What I will do with what I learned:

151.   "God desires that we are ambitious and confident to take on our visions (projects, goals, dreams, purposes, etc.) and accomplish them."

152.   "Whether divine or worldly, ambition is always accompanied by confidence."

153.   "An ambitious and confident general is likely to win the war."

Quotable Action

◀ What I learned from the quotes:

▼ What I will do with what I learned:

154. "An ambitious and confident preacher is likely to bring souls into the Kingdom of God."

155. "An ambitious and confident businessperson is likely to make profit."

156. "An ambitious and confident politician is likely to win an election."

Quotable Action

◀ What I learned from the quotes:

▼ What I will do with what I learned:

157.　"If we have no ambition, are not confident, are afraid of anything that frightens us, and lack courage, we may not achieve greatly in this life, and probably, in the one to come."

158.　"Confidence equation: ambition + confidence + fearlessness + courage + the presence of God = invincibility.

Be ambitious.
Be determined.
Be fearless.
Be courageous.
Be confident."

Quotable Action

◀ What I learned from the quotes:

▼ What I will do with what I learned:

159. "Confidence is tamed ambition, a drive strong enough to be overcome not even by death."

160. "It is alright to have a drive in life as long as it is measured, leveled and ethically managed."

161. "Drive produces confidence which is essential to performance and goal realization."

Quotable Action

◄ What I learned from the quotes:

▼ What I will do with what I learned:

162.　"Rule of Constants and
　　　Variables #1: Science,
　　　mathematics and to some
　　　extent, philosophy, operate by
　　　some predictions based on
　　　identified conditions or
　　　relationships."

Quotable Action

◀ What I learned from the quotes:

▼ What I will do with what I learned:

163.   "Rule of Constants and Variables #2: At the core are two relationships, constants and variables. Constants indicate those factors that don't change with time or circumstances; and variables, are those that change with time and circumstances."

Quotable Action

◀ What I learned from the quotes:

▼ What I will do with what I learned:

164. "Rule of Constants and Variables #3: When determining speed, they look at the constant of distance and manipulate its relationship with the variable of time."

Quotable Action

◀ What I learned from the quotes:

▼ What I will do with what I learned:

165. "Rule of Constants and Variables #4: How these two are related and the conditions presented may determine how a scientist predicts the rate of speed. The same goes for predictions of weather, seasons and geographical movements and structures by meteorologists, of planetary or spatial explorations by astrologers, etc."

Quotable Action

◀ What I learned from the quotes:

▼ What I will do with what I learned:

166. "Rule of Constants and Variables #5: Life is also made up of constants and variables. Those things about and around you that you cannot change are constants, and those you can change or manipulate, are variables."

Quotable Action

◀ What I learned from the quotes:

▼ What I will do with what I learned:

167.   "Rule of Constants and Variables #6: Confidence is a science. To build confidence, identify and major in your constants (such as personality, height, weight, tribe, color of skin, etc.) and *acceptance* of these factors must be total and unequivocal."

Quotable Action

◄ What I learned from the quotes:

▼ What I will do with what I learned:

168. "Rule of Constants and Variables #7: Reflect on your variables (such as nationality, poverty or richness, education or lack of it, marriage or singleness, employment or lack of it, happiness or sadness, hope or disappointment, goals and dreams, etc.) and *tolerance* of these and manipulation of them depends on how they relate to the constants."

Quotable Action

◀ What I learned from the quotes:

▼ What I will do with what I learned:

169.　"Rule of Constants and Variables #8: You must *accept* the fact that you are White or Black (constant) but refuse to be poor (variable); or accept the fact that you have a reserved personality (constant) but choose to be an excellent speaker or preacher (variables), etc."

Quotable Action

◀ What I learned from the quotes:

▼ What I will do with what I learned:

170.   "Rule of Constants and Variables #9: Accept things about you that you can't change and improve within their limits; but decide to manipulate or change or adjust or operate on the variables (things you can change) to make them fit or adapt to the things you can't change (or constants)."

Quotable Action

◄ What I learned from the quotes:

▼ What I will do with what I learned:

171.   "Rule of Constants and Variables #10: The biggest mistake and which will be the cause of anxiety, stress, depression, unfulfillment, misery, disillusionment, and even death, is to reverse the order; trying to change constants and major in variables."

Quotable Action

◄ What I learned from the quotes:

▼ What I will do with what I learned:

172.　"Rule of Constants and Variables #11: Those who reverse the order of constants and variables may be extremely unhappy in life. They will, probably, spend a great deal of their lives sad, lonely, moody, unfulfilled and even irritable."

Quotable Action

◄ What I learned from the quotes:

▼ What I will do with what I learned:

173.   "Rule of Constants and Variables #12: Self-blame is a sign of reversal of constant and variable order. Such people who do so will likely blame themselves for everything, and sometimes even blame God for who they are (instead of appreciating just the way they are and giving God the praise)."

Quotable Action

◀ What I learned from the quotes:

▼ What I will do with what I learned:

174.   "Rule of Constants and Variables #13: Waste is a characteristic of reversal of constants and variables. Such people may waste time, money, energy trying to 'measure up to the standard' set for them by the culture around them."

Quotable Action

◀ What I learned from the quotes:

▼ What I will do with what I learned:

175.   "Rule of Constants and Variables #14: In one's constant, one is more and naturally comfortable. Within that natural, comfort zone, one can achieve greatly and be at liberty."

Quotable Action

◀ What I learned from the quotes:

▼ What I will do with what I learned:

176.   "Rule of Constants and
Variables #15: The definition
of the *ideal* (ideal weight,
height, educational level, right
color, etc.) is usually a
construct of the commercially,
profit-motivated and culturally
dominant groups, because by
creating a fake ideal standard,
they could control trade,
supply-and-demand and create
an appetite for the mundane."

Quotable Action

◄ What I learned from the quotes:

▼ What I will do with what I learned:

177.   "Rule of Constants and Variables #16: The fake ideals aim at generating sales and domination, no matter who gets injured (mentally or culturally) in the process."

Quotable Action

◀ What I learned from the quotes:

▼ What I will do with what I learned:

178.   "Rule of Constants and Variables #17: Variety is the currency that the Creator used to design His creation – thus, not all flowers are pink or blue or red or white or black or yellow or brown, and not all weights are big or small, and not all heights are tall or short, and not all races are Black or White, and not all countries are in Europe or America or Asia or Africa, and not all things are the same."

Quotable Action

◀ What I learned from the quotes:

▼ What I will do with what I learned:

179. "Rule of Constants and Variables #18: Variety brings a synergy of diversified excellence, where one kind blends with another to produce a rhythmically buoyant and flamboyant end-product."

Quotable Action

◀ What I learned from the quotes:

▼ What I will do with what I learned:

180.   "Rule of Constants and Variables #19: The core of desire is, therefore, not homogeneity, but complementarity. And as such, a person should be preoccupied with the improvement, within their kind and not imitate another kind, of who they are."

Quotable Action

◀ What I learned from the quotes:

▼ What I will do with what I learned:

181. "Rule of Constants and Variables #20: The goal of improvement within one's kind is the essence of creativity."

182. "Rule of Constants and Variables #21: Therefore, if one wants to be happy with and about who they are, they ought to accept who they are, first and foremost, and then work within the prevailing variables to improve their core, which is the constant."

Quotable Action

◀ What I learned from the quotes:

▼ What I will do with what I learned:

183.   "Rule of Constants and Variables #22: One should not desire to be short (constant) if they are tall (constant) or to be short if they are tall. But within their kind, they must improve themselves."

184.   "Rule of Constants and Variables #23: There is a scientific concept of *entropy*. In a layman's language, entropy defines a state of disorder if no external forces improve upon something."

Quotable Action

◀ What I learned from the quotes:

▼ What I will do with what I learned:

185.   "Rule of Constants and Variables #24: A thing or matter, intrinsically, gradually declines into disorder if not tended after a long while. If you leave a car in a garage locked up in its top-of-the-cut cleanliness, when you return after a long while, you will find that it has gathered dirt."

Quotable Action

◀ What I learned from the quotes:

▼ What I will do with what I learned:

186.   "Rule of Constants and Variables #25: Thus, sustainability comes with use and not neglect."

187.   "Rule of Constants and Variables #26: If you are a White person (constant) and you don't tend to your skin (variable – dirty or clean), it will decay, and that same thing goes for a Black person."

Quotable Action

◄ What I learned from the quotes:

▼ What I will do with what I learned:

188. "Rule of Constants and Variables #27: Foolishness is attempting to be Black or White if you can't appreciate and accept the constant factor about you, namely, the color of your skin."

Quotable Action

◀ What I learned from the quotes:

▼ What I will do with what I learned:

189. "Rule of Constants and Variables #28: Like driving, if you stay within your lane, you are likely to arrive alive. If you want to drive in another's lane, you may end up unhappy, sad or dead."

190. "Rule of Constants and Variables #29: If you can be, and appreciate, and accept who you are and stay in your natural lane, you will increase the chances of being happy and confident in life."

Quotable Action

◀ What I learned from the quotes:

▼ What I will do with what I learned:

191.   "Rule of Constants and Variables #30: In your constant, you are an original, and a standard to yourself. You improve, limit or exceed your standard on your own terms. You are happiest and at your best when you are who you are. That's the source of all your confidence."

Quotable Action

◀ What I learned from the quotes:

▼ What I will do with what I learned:

192. "It's better to set an expected end and then work it backwards than to work forward in order to set a goal."

193. "The expectations of bad people eventually come to nothing."

194. "Let God put in your mind and heart what to expect."

Quotable Action

◀ What I learned from the quotes:

▼ What I will do with what I learned:

195. "Expectation requires preparation – spread your hands wide if you expect to receive."

196. "Accord your vision in line with your earnest expectation and hope."

197. "Be careful about nothing; but in everything by prayer and supplication with thanksgiving let your requests be made known unto God."[7]

---

[7] Philippians 4:6

Quotable Action

◄ What I learned from the quotes:

▼ What I will do with what I learned:

198.   "Knowledge and wisdom are necessary to strengthening one's expectations."

199.   "Action must proceed from expectation."

200.   "Decree that which you expect, and it shall be established for you."

Quotable Action

◀ What I learned from the quotes:

▼ What I will do with what I learned:

201.   "Expectation is not an end; it is a process that leads to a hopeful end."

202.   "Unfulfilled expectations cause suffering" (Buddha).

203.   "Learn to love without condition. Talk without bad intention. Give without any reason. And most of all, care for people without any expectation" (Buddha).

Quotable Action

◄ What I learned from the quotes:

▼ What I will do with what I learned:

204.　"I am as my slave expects me to be" (Islam).

205.　"If you expect nothing from somebody you are never disappointed. Blessed is he who expects nothing, for he shall never be disappointed. When you stop expecting people to be perfect, you can like them for who they are" (Alexander Pope).

Quotable Action

◀ What I learned from the quotes:

▼ What I will do with what I learned:

206.   "If our expectations, if our fondest prayers and dreams, are not realized then we should all bear in mind that the greatest glory of living lies in never falling but in rising every time you fall" (Nelson Mandela).

207.   "To wish was to hope, and to hope was to expect" (Jane Austen).

Quotable Action

◀ What I learned from the quotes:

▼ What I will do with what I learned:

208.   "We were promised
    sufferings. They were part of
    the program. We were even
    told, 'Blessed are they that
    mourn,' and I accept it. I've
    got nothing that I hadn't
    bargained for. Of course, it is
    different when the thing
    happens to oneself, not to
    others, and in reality, not
    imagination" (C.S. Lewis).

Quotable Action

◀ What I learned from the quotes:

▼ What I will do with what I learned:

209. "It takes three to make love, not two: you, your spouse, and God. Without God people only succeed in bringing out the worst in one another. Lovers who have nothing else to do but love each other soon find there is nothing else. Without a central loyalty life is unfinished" (Fulton J. Sheen).

Quotable Action

◄ What I learned from the quotes:

▼ What I will do with what I learned:

210.   "Stop expecting to be understood by people who have little understanding of themselves" (African Proverb).

Quotable Action

◄ What I learned from the quotes:

▼ What I will do with what I learned:

ABOUT THE AUTHOR

Best Selling Author, Charles Mwewa (LLB; BA Law; BA Ed; LLM), is a prolific researcher, poet, novelist, lawyer, law professor and Christian apologist and intercessor. Mwewa has written no less than 85 books and counting in every genre and has exhibited his works at prestigious expos like the Ottawa International Book Expo and is the winner of the Coppa Awards for his signature publication, *Zambia: Struggles of My People.*
Mwewa and his family live in the Canadian Capital City of Ottawa.

SELECTED BOOKS BY THIS AUTHOR

1. *ZAMBIA: Struggles of My People (First and Second Editions)*
2. *10 FINANCIAL & WEALTH ATTITUDES TO AVOID*
3. *10 STRATEGIES TO DEFEAT STRESS AND DEPRESSION: Creating an Internal Safeguard against Stress and Depression*
4. *100+ REASONS TO READ BOOKS*
5. *A CASE FOR AFRICA?S LIBERTY: The Synergistic Transformation of Africa and the West into First-World Partnerships*
6. *A PANDEMIC POETRY, COVID-19*
7. *ALLERGIC TO CORRUPTION: The Legacy of President Michael Sata of Zambia*
8. *BOOK ABOUT SOMETHING: On Ultimate Purpose*
9. *CAMPAIGN FOR AFRICA: A Provocative Crusade for the Economic and Humanitarian Decolonization of Africa*
10. *CHAMPIONS: Application of Common Sense and Biblical Motifs to Succeed in Both Worlds*
11. *CORONAVIRUS PRAYERS*
12. *HH IS THE RIGHT MAN FOR ZAMBIA: And Other Acclaimed Articles on Zambia and Africa*
13. *I BOW: 3500 Prayer Lines of Inspiration & Intercession from the Heart: Volume One*
14. *INTERUNIVERSALISM IN A NUTSHELL: For Iranian Refugee Claimants*
15. *LAW & GRACE: An Expository Study in the Rudiments of Sin and Truth*
16. *LAWS OF INFLUENCE: 7even Lessons in Transformational Leadership*
17. *LOVE IDEAS IN COVID PANDEMIC TIMES:*

INDEX

www.ingramcontent.com/pod-product-compliance
Lightning Source LLC
Chambersburg PA
CBHW050116280326
41933CB00010B/1126